FILIPINOS

IMMIGRATION
AND THE
AMERICAN WAY OF LIFE

Geologically speaking, the continent of North America is very old. The people who live here, by comparison, are new arrivals. Even the first settlers, the American Indians who came here from Asia about 35,000 years ago, are fairly new, not to speak of the first European settlers who came by ship or the refugees who flew in yesterday. Whenever they came, they were all immigrants. How all these immigrants live together today to form one society has been compared to the making of a mosaic. A mosaic is a picture formed from many different pieces. Thus, in America, many groups of people—from African Americans or Albanians to Tibetans or Welsh—live side by side. This human mosaic was put together by the immigrants themselves, with courage, hard work, and luck. Each group of immigrants has its own history and its own reasons for coming to America. Immigrants from different regions have their own way of creating communities for themselves and their children. In creating those communities, they not only keep elements of their own heritage alive, but also enrich further the fabric of American society. Each book in *Recent American Immigrants* will examine a part of this human mosaic up close. The books will look at some of the most recent arrivals to find out what they are like and how they fit into the whole mosaic.

Recent American Immigrants

FILIPINOS

Jodine Mayberry

Consultant
Roger Daniels, Department of History
University of Cincinnati

Franklin Watts
New York • London • Toronto • Sydney

Developed by: Ω **Visual Education Corporation**
Princeton, NJ

Cover: Alain Evrard/Photo Researchers, Inc.

Photo Credits: p. 3 (L) Philip Jon Bailey/Jerobam, Inc.; p. 3 (M)
Frank Siteman/Stock Boston; p. 3 (R) Tony Jalandoni/Monkmeyer
Press Photography; p. 9 Peter Gridley/FPG International; p. 10 The
Bettmann Archive; p. 11 D. & J. Heaton/Stock Boston; p. 12 Culver
Pictures, Inc.; p. 14 Historical Pictures Service-Chicago; p. 15 The
Bettmann Archive; p. 16 Historical Pictures Service-Chicago; p. 18
Demonstration Project for Asian Americans, Seattle; p. 20 The
Library of Congress; p. 24 Demonstration Project for Asian
Americans, Seattle; p. 27 Demonstration Project for Asian
Americans, Seattle; p. 29 Demonstration Project for Asian
Americans, Seattle; p. 33 Demonstration Project for Asian
Americans, Seattle; p. 37 The Bettmann Archive; p. 38 Alain
Evrard/Photo Researchers, Inc.; p. 44 Norris Klesman/Picture
Group, Inc.; p. 45 Alberto Garcia/Picture Group, Inc.; p. 46 United
States Navy; p. 48 Wernher Krutein/Jeroboam, Inc.; p. 49 Archives of
Labor and Urban Affairs, Wayne State University; p. 51
Demonstration Project for Asian Americans, Seattle; p. 52 G. Monty
Manibog; p. 53 The Atlanta Ballet; p. 54 Dorothy L. Cordova/
Demonstration Project for Asian Americans; p. 55 Joe Viesti/Viesti
Associates, Inc.; p. 56 (T) Rene Ner; p. 56 (B) Joe Carini/Pacific
Ocean Stock; p. 57 Rene Ner; p. 59 Rene Ner; p. 60 Anthony
Jalandoni/Monkmeyer Press Photography; p. 61 Joe Carini/Pacific
Ocean Stock

Library of Congress Cataloging-in-Publication Data

Mayberry, Jodine,
Filipinos/Jodine Mayberry
p.   cm. — (Recent American immigrants)
Includes bibliographical references (p.   ).
Summary: Discusses Filipino immigrants to America, their reasons for
coming, their lifestyles, and their contributions to their new country.
ISBN 0-531-10978-X
1. Filipino Americans — Juvenile literature. 2. United States — Emigration
and immigration — Juvenile literature. 3. Philippines — Emigration and
immigration — Juvenile literature. [1. Filipino Americans.] I. Title.
II. Series: Recent American immigrants.
E184.F4G67   1990
973'.049921 — dc20   90-12274 CIP AC

Contents

CHINA

PACIFIC
OCEAN

South
China
Sea

LUZON

Manila ⭑

PHILIPPINES

VIETNAM

MINDORO

SAMAR

PANAY   CEBU

LEYTE

NEGROS

PALAWAN

MINDANAO

I N D O N E S I A

| 0 | 250 | 500 miles |
| 0 | 250 | 500 kilometers |

The Philippines to 1900

THE PHILIPPINES

The Philippines is a beautiful, tropical land of sea and mountains. It is an archipelago, or chain, of 7,000 islands in the Pacific Ocean. The islands of the Philippines are actually the tops of undersea mountains and volcanoes. There are still twelve active volcanoes in the Philippines and hundreds of inactive ones. You can find the Philippines on a world map by looking southeast of China and east of Vietnam.

The two largest islands in the Philippines are Mindanao, at the southern end of the chain, and Luzon, at the northern end. Most people who have come to the United States from the Philippines were Ilocanos. They live on the northern half of Luzon. The second-largest group of immigrants came from the Visayan Islands, which include Cebu, Samar, and Leyte, on the eastern edge of the Philippines.

For most of its long history, the Philippines was not one nation. It was merely a group of islands where many different peoples lived. Each ethnic group had its own territory, spoke its own language, and followed its own customs. The people in the interior of the islands lived by farming. Those along the coasts lived by fishing and trading.

The Philippines was seized by Spain in the 1500s and remained under Spain's rule for 350 years. For the first half of the twentieth century, it was a territory of the United States. Only in 1946 did the Philippines become independent.

As you will read later in these pages, the Spanish had a tremendous influence on the people of the Philippines, who are called *Filipinos*. Most of these people adopted the Spanish language, customs, and religion, Roman Catholicism. The United States also greatly influenced the Filipinos. Many learned English and acquired educations that enabled them to become leaders in Filipino society. Because the Philippines was an American possession, hundreds of thousands of Filipinos were able to come to the United States. They went to school and work here.

ETHNIC ORIGINS

The earliest group of people to arrive in the Philippines were the *Negritos* ("little blacks" in Spanish). They came to the islands about 25,000 years ago. They were small people who were primarily hunters and gatherers. Today the Negritos are a tiny minority group in the Philippines.

The Malays came to the Philippines as early as 7,000 years ago. They came from Southeast Asia and Indonesia. Waves of Malays kept coming for hundreds of years. The largest migration may have occurred in the thirteenth century. They are of medium height and have brown skin. The Malays were farmers and fishers. They are now the largest racial group in the Philippines.

From about A.D. 1000, Chinese and Arab traders began visiting the Philippines regularly. The traders brought pottery, woven cloth, jewelry, tools, and weapons to the islanders. They traded these goods for pearls, rice, coral, fish, and native handicrafts. The Arabs introduced Islam to the peoples of Mindanao and other southern islands. The large Muslim minority group, usually called *Moros,* in the Philippines is still dominant on those islands.

A view of the Philippines: Lake Taal on Luzon, south of Manila

People in the Philippines speak more than eighty dialects. Most of them can be classified under eight major language groups. The national language is Pilipino. It is studied in all Philippine schools. Pilipino is based on Tagalog. That is the language spoken in the area around Manila, the chief city of the Philippines.

In addition to Tagalog, other major languages include Visayan and Ilocano. Nearly half of the Filipino people speak Visayan. Most Visayans in America speak a dialect called Cebuano. Only about 15 percent of Filipinos speak Ilocano. However, it is the most common language of Filipino immigrants because so many of them have come from that region.

Because of the introduction of American education early in the twentieth century, most educated Filipinos speak English also. As in India, in the Philippines English is the unifying language among peoples who speak many different languages.

Filipinos identify themselves by the island or region they come from, the language they speak, and their family membership. These have always been more important to them than their national identity. They customarily live together in *barrios* (villages or city neighborhoods) in large family groups. The family groups usually include parents, grandparents, aunts, uncles, cousins, and relatives by marriage.

THE EARLY HISTORY OF THE PHILIPPINES

In 1521, Ferdinand Magellan became the first European to reach the Philippines. He was making the first sea voyage around the world. Like Columbus, Magellan was looking for a new route to Asia. His voyage proved the world was round.

Magellan landed on Samar on March 15. He claimed the Philippines for Spain. Magellan was killed by followers of Datu Lapu-Lapu, a local leader, on the Philippine island of Mactan and buried there. Only twenty-two of Magellan's men returned to Spain. A few years later, the islands were named after King Philip II of Spain.

In 1565, Philip II sent Miguel Lopez de Legazpi to establish a permanent colony on the Philippines. Lopez founded Manila in 1571.

The Spanish established large plantations where they grew sugarcane. They also developed a very profitable trade with Mexico, which was also a Spanish possession. They purchased goods from India and China and shipped them to Mexico in the "Manila galleons." These ships made the long annual voyage from Manila to Mexico and then back to Manila. The galleons came back loaded with Mexican silver and goods from the New World.

Philip II (1527–1598), king of Spain, ruled over a vast empire that encircled the globe.

INFLUENCES ON FILIPINO LIFE

The Spanish   The Filipinos adopted the language and customs of Spain as a result of the long Spanish rule. Some Filipino women married Spanish men and had children of mixed ancestry. In 1849, the Filipinos were required to take Spanish surnames. That is why so many Filipinos have names like *Gomez, Reyes,* and *Vargas.*

The Chinese   The Chinese also influenced Filipinos. Many of the traders intermarried and settled in the islands. They became bankers, merchants, and business owners.

The Church   When the Spanish arrived, they brought Roman Catholic priests, friars, and nuns with them. They quickly set about converting the Filipinos into Christians. They built churches, schools, and roads. They established Christian traditions, such as the Feast of Santo Niño ("Holy Child"). It is still a popular Filipino holiday.

The priests controlled the educational system in the Philippines. Only the richest families could afford to send their children to college or overseas to study. The majority of Filipinos were too poor to educate their children.

Manila Cathedral, located within the original walled city built by the Spanish

FILIPINO REACTION TO SPANISH RULE

Under Spanish rule, most Filipinos could not get an education or own land. They had few legal rights, and most were very poor. Many became tenant farmers for rich Spanish landholders. That meant they had to rent land or give the landowners a part of the crops they grew. The Filipinos became very unhappy with Spanish rule. In the nineteenth century, they rebelled against the Spanish, as did most other Spanish possessions.

The Filipinos wanted to establish their own nation. One of the leaders of the nationalist movement was Dr. José Protasio Rizal. Rizal wanted the Spanish to provide education for everyone. He wrote two novels, *Noli Me Tangere (Don't Touch Me)* and *El Filibusterismo (The Revolutionary)*, that inspired the nationalist movement.

In 1896, an armed uprising broke out against the Spanish. Rizal was opposed to violence. He had nothing to do with the uprising. Nevertheless, the Spanish arrested and executed him. He became the Philippines' first national hero. Filipinos still revere him today, just as we honor George Washington.

**José Protasio Rizal
(1861–1896)**

THE SPANISH-AMERICAN WAR

After Rizal's death, the Filipino uprising continued. In 1898, Filipino freedom fighters, led by Emilio Aguinaldo, established a temporary government in the Philippines. In the meantime, the United States had also gone to war with Spain.

Although the United States and Spain went to war in 1898 over Cuba, the United States also attacked the Spanish in the Philippines. On May 1, 1898, Admiral George B. Dewey sailed into Manila harbor. His fleet defeated the Spanish fleet moored in the harbor. Aguinaldo brought his troops to help Dewey. He was convinced that the United States would help the Filipinos gain their independence. After the war, however, the United States bought the Philippines, Guam, and Puerto Rico from Spain for $20 million.

In the United States, some people opposed the U.S. annexation, or takeover, of the Philippines. They felt it was wrong for America to own another country. This was imperialism, they said. Many of America's leaders, however, were in favor of annexation. Business leaders saw the Philippines as a source of valuable raw materials such as timber and hemp. Some politicians claimed falsely that all Filipinos were savages and that they were inferior to white people. They felt that the Filipinos needed America's help to become civilized.

President William McKinley was one of the American leaders who believed that the Filipinos were inferior savages. Here is how he justified the annexation of the Philippines: "We could not give them back to Spain—that would be cowardly and dishonorable . . . we could not leave them to themselves—they were unfit for self-government; and . . . there was nothing left for us to do but take them all, and to educate the Filipinos, and . . . civilize and Christianize them."

McKinley seemed not to realize that most Filipinos already were Christian.

THE PHILIPPINE-AMERICAN WAR

Aguinaldo and his followers felt angry and betrayed. They felt the Philippines had traded one set of rulers for another. They tried to keep the United States from taking over their islands. The Philippine-American War lasted several years. By the time the war was over, the United States had sent 126,000 troops and spent $170 million to subdue the Filipinos.

About 4,000 American soldiers lost their lives in the war. Filipino losses were much higher. Some 16,000 rebels and 100,000 to 200,000 civilians died from war-related causes. Some historians put the number as high as 600,000. The United States put thousands of Filipinos in prison camps. This was to keep them from joining the rebels. Many of these people died of starvation and disease. The United States had also been accused of war crimes, of torturing and massacring many Filipino soldiers and civilians during the war.

Aguinaldo was captured in 1901. He took an oath of allegiance to the United States. That marked the formal end of the Philippine-American War. However, guerrilla bands kept fighting for several more years. The Moros in Mindanao were not subdued until 1913.

Emilio Aguinaldo (1869–1964), long-lived Filipino leader

14

William Howard Taft (1857–1930) greets a Filipino leader, ca. 1905.

GOVERNOR GENERAL TAFT

In 1903, after the Philippine-American War, William Howard Taft became the first civilian governor general of the Philippines. He was an efficient administrator who later became president of the United States (1909–1913). Taft's opinion of Filipinos was similar to McKinley's. He believed they needed U.S. help to learn how to govern themselves. He once referred to them as "our little brown brothers."

The official policy of the United States was to prepare the Philippines to become an independent nation. Gradually, the United States introduced democratic forms such as elections and legislatures to the Filipinos. The United States wanted to provide education to as many Filipinos as possible. It sent hundreds of teachers to the Philippines and opened schools everywhere. The teachers used American textbooks and taught about democracy and American ideals in the schools. The government required that English be taught in all schools.

The government also built hospitals, roads, water systems, and other public works to improve the lives of the people. It did little, however, to change the economic system. Only a handful of wealthy Filipinos owned the land and the factories. The vast majority of Filipinos remained poor and landless.

**Many Filipinos went first to Hawaii to work on
sugarcane plantations like this one.**

Early Immigration to the United States, 1900–1920

The earliest Filipinos to come to America were small numbers of crewmen from the Manila galleons. They came from Mexico in the eighteenth century and migrated to Louisiana. Most seemed to have lived in and around New Orleans. A few Filipinos also were laborers in Hawaii and the Pacific Northwest. Some were cannery workers in Alaska.

U.S. NATIONALS

Filipinos did not begin to immigrate to the United States in large numbers until the Philippines became a U.S. possession. Then, as citizens of a U.S. territory, Filipinos had the status of "American nationals." This meant they enjoyed the protection of the U.S. government and could travel freely to the United States. However, they were not American citizens. Further, they could not become naturalized citizens. The naturalization law passed just after the Civil War permitted only "white persons" and "persons of African descent" to become naturalized citizens. However, thanks to the Fourteenth Amendment to the U.S. Constitution, all persons born in the United States were automatically citizens. Therefore, the children born in the United States of Filipino and other Asian-born parents were full citizens.

PENSIONADOS

Part of Governor General Taft's educational program for the
Philippines was to send Filipino students to the United States
for college educations. The territorial government provided

Filipino students in the United States early in the 1900s

scholarships, or "pensions," for the students. These students became known as *pensionados*.

The pensionados were among the first Filipinos to come to the United States. In 1903, the government sent 103 students to American colleges and universities. Most of them studied medicine, engineering, agriculture, and education. In 1907, 187 pensionados came to the United States and enrolled in forty-seven schools and colleges.

Altogether, only a few hundred pensionados came to the United States. They were not permanent immigrants. They were all supposed to return home and repay the government by using their skills in the Philippines. By 1910, most of the students had completed their studies and returned home. They became political and business leaders in their communities.

A NEW WAVE OF STUDENTS

The pensionados inspired other Filipinos to go to college in the United States in the dozen or so years following 1908. These students wanted to study sciences, social sciences, and technology. The new group of students did not receive government scholarships, however. They and their parents had to pay for their educations.

The students found life hard in America. In school they had learned about equality, but they found that Americans did not really treat them as equals. They were discriminated against as foreigners and persons of color.

Since it was very expensive for students to live in the United States, some soon ran out of money. They had to quit school and take low-paying jobs. Despite these hardships, many students completed their studies and returned home. Like the pensionados, they too became leaders in Filipino society. Many others remained in the United States permanently.

FILIPINOS IN HAWAII

Like the Philippines, the Hawaiian Islands were an American possession. Many Hawaiians owned large plantations where they grew sugarcane and pineapple. These plantations required many field laborers. The landowners wanted workers who would accept low wages. At first, the landowners imported Chinese and Japanese workers. However, the U.S. government halted the immigration of these Asian laborers by 1908. The Hawaiian landowners then looked to another American possession, the Philippines, for workers.

Hawaii began importing Filipino laborers in 1909. It sent recruiters to the Philippines to find workers. The first Filipinos to sign up were a few hundred Tagalogs and Visayans. Soon, however, the plantation owners started recruiting Ilocanos from the rural areas of northern Luzon.

Most Filipinos who went to Hawaii were young men from very poor families. To them Hawaii was "a land of glory." They thought they would work on the Hawaiian plantations for a few years. Then they would return to their villages as wealthy men.

By 1930, Filipinos were one of the largest ethnic groups in Hawaii. Between 1909 and 1940, more than 125,000 Filipinos immigrated to Hawaii.

A Filipino worker in a Hawaiian pineapple field

The HSPA   The Hawaiian plantation owners who began recruiting Filipino workers in 1909 belonged to an organization called the Hawaiian Sugar Plantation Association (HSPA). The HSPA sent recruiting agents to the Philippines every year. In the villages, they showed propaganda movies that reported the fine lives of plantation workers in Hawaii. They promised the Filipinos they would be paid two dollars a day (a promise that was not kept). That was a fortune to most Filipinos. At that time, the average Filipino could earn an amount equal to only about fifteen cents a day. The HSPA recruited more than 11,000 Filipinos in 1925. After that, so many Filipinos signed up on their own to work in the cane fields that the HSPA did not need to recruit any more.

The HSPA required that each worker sign a contract promising to work in the sugarcane fields for three years. In exchange, the workers would receive their wages, free housing, water, fuel, and medical care. However, they had to buy their own food. This cost them a large portion of their pay.

The Sakadas   The workers who were recruited by the HSPA were known as *Sakadas*. This term was coined by Filipinos. It was used only in Hawaii to mean an agricultural worker. And these workers were really indentured workers. Indentured workers made a contract to work for an employer for a specified period of time.

They were a distinct group of people in Hawaii and to them we trace the history of the Filipinos in Hawaii. I use their term rather than impose another term, "contract laborers," or whatever, because that was how they identified themselves, and proudly at that.

—Ruben Alcantara

As quoted in Fred Cordova, *Filipinos: Forgotten Asian Americans* (Dubuque, Iowa: Kendall, 1983), p. 29.

Life in Hawaii   Life in the Hawaiian cane fields was very hard for the Filipinos. Because they were small and worked fast, they were thought to be ideally suited for performing stoop labor. This meant that they worked hunched over all day planting, cutting, and carrying sugarcane or pineapples. This was painful, backbreaking work. Women and children worked right along with the men.

The Filipinos lived in separate camps. They were isolated from the white owners and from other workers. Most of the Filipino workers were unmarried men. Many of those who were married did not bring their families with them. They all expected to go back home in a few short years. In any case, the plantation owners discouraged the Sakadas from starting families. They did not want to pay for houses and schools for Filipino families.

The Filipinos were treated as the lowliest of workers by their bosses, often Spanish or Portuguese overseers, called *lunas*. Filipinos were given the hardest, most unpleasant jobs. Sometimes the lunas would beat them with sticks. The lunas gave the Chinese and Japanese better work assignments than they gave the Filipinos. Because the Chinese and Japanese were there first, they looked down on newcomers.

The Sakadas experienced racism and poverty as emigrants from their own country. They had no legal rights. They could not vote. And they could not get an education. The HSPA deliberately recruited uneducated Filipinos to work in the cane fields. Unlike the students, they were brought in to work, not to learn.

> *The sugarcane cutters [earn] one dollar a*
> *day. They burn the sugar fields first at night.*
> *In the morning they all go out clean. When*
> *they come back, they all look [filthy].*
> —*Becky Ebat Javanillo*

As quoted in Cordova, p. 30.

Sending Money Home   Despite their hardships, many Sakadas were able to fulfill their dreams. They worked hard, saved their money, and went home. Between 1909 and 1930, an estimated 55,000 Sakadas returned home. Many Filipinos regularly sent money from Hawaii to their families.

The money usually went to the Sakadas' extended families. Filipinos had a strong tradition of loyalty. They were expected to help support the family group. In turn, if they were hungry or needy, the group would help them. When the Sakadas sent money home, the group used it to pay taxes and to purchase houses and farmland for family members. Some money went to educate the children in the group.

When a Sakada's contract was up, he or she was free to go. Many chose to remain in Hawaii. Some went on to the U.S. mainland to look for other work. However, in the 1930s, economic conditions were poor everywhere. The Great Depression threw many people out of work in Hawaii and on the mainland. The plantation owners no longer needed new Filipino workers. Of those who remained in Hawaii, many left the cane fields to look for better jobs. Some joined labor unions and tried to improve working conditions in the fields. However, unions were not fully effective in Hawaii until the mid-1940s. Whatever they did, the Filipinos have made a lasting contribution to the society and economy of Hawaii.

> *What I see of the Sakada story is that over-triumph of the human will. If you ask about their future, old age, for instance, they will tell me, "I have conquered a lot of changes in the past, and I am confident that I will be able to conquer any kind of challenge." This is essentially the story of the Sakadas.*
>
> —*Ruben Alcantara*

As quoted in Cordova, p. 35.

During the 1920s, many Filipinos became agricultural workers on the U.S. mainland.

Filipino Immigration, 1920–1940

COMING TO THE MAINLAND

Most of the first Filipinos to come to the U.S. mainland had first gone to Hawaii. From 1923 on, they began to arrive in large numbers directly from the Philippines. Filipinos who came to the United States called themselves *Pinoys,* a slang term used only in the United States to mean a Filipino who lived here. Life was still very hard in the Philippines. Poor Filipinos were shut out of jobs and schools. Few could afford to buy land.

There were virtually no opportunities to get ahead and rise out of poverty in the Philippines. But in the American-run schools, generations of Filipino youngsters were learning that America was the "land of opportunity." In America, they learned, they could get good-paying jobs or go to school and learn a profession.

The U.S. government had excluded Chinese laborers from immigrating to the United States in 1882. In 1908, it also excluded most Japanese laborers. These actions were based on the strong anti-Asian sentiment in the United States at that time. These measures created a need for more agricultural workers in the American West. Filipinos eagerly filled that need. There was no limit on how many Filipinos could come to America. This was because the Philippines was an American territory and Filipinos were U.S. nationals, although not citizens. In 1920, the U.S. census reported that there were 5,603 Filipino Americans. "Filipino American" describes any person of Filipino origin who is not a casual visitor and lives in the United States. By 1930, the number had grown to 45,208. Most Filipino Americans lived in California. New York, Illinois, Washington, and Oregon also had large Filipino populations.

Three-fourths of Filipino immigrants were single men or men who had left their families in the Philippines. They led a very nomadic life in the United States. They followed the crop harvests or performed other seasonal work. They lived in migrant camps or in the poorest parts of towns. In some big cities, they often lived in or near the Chinatowns.

Like their fellow Filipinos in Hawaii, those who came to the mainland experienced racism and discrimination for the first time. They had learned in school that in America "all men are created equal." However, when they came to the United States, they were resented and treated as inferiors because they were not white. Many Filipinos were very disillusioned and wanted to go back home.

WHERE FILIPINOS WORKED

Service Jobs   Filipinos quickly gained a reputation for being obedient, polite, and hardworking. These qualities made them very desirable as service workers in homes, restaurants, and hotels. They took jobs as valets, janitors, porters, bellboys, yardboys, elevator operators, dishwashers, and houseboys. People called them "boy" regardless of how old they were. They were not regarded as "men," as equals.

Alaskan Canneries   Thousands of Filipinos took jobs in Alaskan salmon canneries during the summer months. They would work in the factories twelve to eighteen hours a day cleaning and packing salmon.

Cannery workers in Ekuk, Alaska, 1926

Worked in the ship unloading salmon cans, at $.75 an hour. It was my first time in America to work. Worked exactly ten hours. Donning the overall for the first time in my life, handling the wheelbarrow, and carrying salmon boxes was a thrill and an unforgettable experience. . . . Was laughing at the easy job and easy money . . . $7.50 for working 10 hours. In the Philippines it takes a month for a policeman to earn that. Such is the better prospect of life in this beautiful country.

As quoted in Harry H. L. Kitano and Roger Daniels, *Asian Americans: Emerging Minorities* (Englewood Cliffs, N.J.: Prentice-Hall, 1988), p. 81.

Filipino cannery workers would go to Seattle or San Francisco during the off season to take service jobs. Often they would fall into debt. Poorly paid to begin with, they also tended to gamble. Then they would borrow money from the cannery contractors. To repay it, they would have to sign on for another canning season.

The Navy and Government   Filipinos have been fine sailors for centuries. Thousands were drawn to the U.S. Merchant Marine and to the U.S. Navy. Despite their reputations as seamen, for many years the navy only allowed them to be mess stewards (waiters). Some Filipinos also found jobs sorting mail in the U.S. Post Office and as Pullman porters on railroads.

Agricultural Jobs   The overwhelming majority of Filipinos worked as field hands on farms. Most were migrant laborers who harvested crops as they ripened in California. They usually worked in crews. Some might have moved from state to state within one growing year. For example, they might have started out harvesting asparagus in California. Then they would move on to Montana to pull sugar beets, and to Idaho to harvest potatoes. Finally, they would end up in Washington or Oregon picking apples. In the winter, they went to Seattle or San Francisco and looked for service jobs.

Working conditions were as hard for farm workers in California as they had been in the Hawaiian cane fields. The Filipinos had to stoop over all day to plant and harvest ground-hugging crops such as lettuce and strawberries. They worked in the blazing sun and swirling dust. Their sweat mixed with the dust and caused their skin to itch unbearably.

The workers lived in camps that were little better than chicken coops. Some lived in tents. They were nearly all men. Married men could not bring their wives or children with them. They were very lonely.

DISCRIMINATION

Filipinos suffered from the same racism and discrimination as the Chinese and Japanese. Because Filipinos were not white, immigration laws barred them from becoming citizens. In fourteen states, they could not marry whites. This was a hardship for the outgoing and lonely Filipinos. The partly Americanized Filipinos had expected to be treated as equals. However, many Americans saw Filipinos as savages, barely a step removed from carrying spears and wearing grass skirts. The Filipinos were taunted and humiliated for their color and race. Landlords refused to rent to them. Restaurants, barbershops, hotels, and theaters refused to serve them. In some cases, people beat them. There were anti-Filipino riots, in which white mobs attacked Filipinos. The worst riot took place in Watsonville, California, in 1930. An angry mob killed one Filipino and injured more than fifty others.

In many ways it was a crime to be a Filipino in California. I came to know the public streets were not free to my people; we were stopped each time . . . a patrolman saw us driving a car. We were suspect each time we were seen with a white woman.
—*Carlos Bulosan*

As quoted in Lorraine Jacobs Crouchett, *Filipinos in California: From the Days of the Galleons to the Present* (El Cerrito, Calif.: Downey Place, 1982), p. 38.

"Positively No Filipinos Allowed" reads the notice on the entrance stairway of this cheap hotel in California.

THE TYDINGS-McDUFFIE ACT

Many people wanted the United States to halt the immigration of Filipinos, who began to compete for jobs during the depression. Since the Philippines was an American possession, Filipinos were not subject to immigration quotas. The only way to cut down on their immigration was to grant the Philippines its independence. Congress passed the Tydings-McDuffie Act in 1934. It established the Philippines as a commonwealth. This meant that the Philippines was still loosely tied to the United States but was more like a separate nation. The law provided that it would gain complete independence after a ten-year transition period. The law also limited immigration of Filipinos to fifty per year.

The Philippine Commonwealth   As a commonwealth, the Philippines won the right to govern itself. The United States, however, retained the right to conduct foreign policy for the Philippines and to establish a defense force to protect it. The Philippines was of strategic importance, and the United States had military bases there.

The Philippines adopted a constitution based on the American constitution. On September 17, 1935, Manuel Quezon was elected the first president of the Philippines. His political rival, Sergio Osmeña, was elected vice president. The two rivals worked well together to try to solve the Philippines' enormous economic problems. They tried to start a land-reform program to give more land to the islands' poor peasants. However, the Philippine Congress was dominated by big landowners. The landowners blocked all attempts at land reform.

In 1935, U.S. General Douglas MacArthur went to the Philippines to begin to organize its defense force. The Philippine government passed a draft law to recruit 40,000 men a year into the military. It also began to build an air force and navy.

A Change in Status in the United States   Under the Tydings-McDuffie Act, the status of Filipinos in the United States changed drastically. For immigration purposes, they were reclassified as aliens. They were no longer able to travel freely between the Philippines and the United States. The immigration quota of fifty was the lowest quota for any nation under the American immigration laws, except for all other Asian nations, which had no quota at all.

30

THE REPATRIATION ACT

Once the Philippines became a commonwealth, many people thought the Filipinos in America would want to go home and help build their new nation. Others simply wanted to expel them. They wanted the immigrants' jobs for white workers. Some Americans thought the Filipinos would be better off back home than in the United States.

Congress could not force Filipino immigrants to go home. Instead, it adopted the Repatriation Act of 1935 to try to entice them to leave. Under the law, the government agreed to give them free passage back to the Philippines on U.S. ships. This law appealed to very few Filipinos. Conditions in the Philippines were even worse than in the United States. There were no jobs to return to. Only about 2,000 went back. Many felt that to go home at the government's expense was to admit that they were failures.

FILIPINO SOCIAL LIFE

Throughout the 1920s and 1930s, the Filipino American population was predominantly male. Many still thought of themselves as sojourners, people who stay for only a short while. They intended to go back home, so they saw no need to bring their wives or sweethearts to the United States. After 1934, they could not bring their families over even if they had wanted to do so. As a result, the young Filipino men in the United States had few women with whom to start families.

Because they moved around so much, the Filipinos did not establish their own ethnic sections in large cities as the Chinese and Japanese did. Nor did they start businesses in the United States like other Asian immigrants. They had come from rural areas in the Philippines and did not have a tradition of being merchants or business owners back home. A few did operate restaurants or barbershops.

After work, the Filipino laborers usually gathered in their camps to sing, talk, and play cards. For excitement they went to the nearest large city. They would frequent dance halls, pool halls, and gambling dens. They also liked to bet on cockfights.

The lonely Filipino men loved to dress in nice clothes and go dancing. They would buy tickets at ten cents each. The tickets allowed them to dance with the women at the dance halls. Each ticket bought one dance or one minute of dancing. Some Filipinos spent their entire week's pay at a dance hall on a Saturday night.

All of these activities—the pool halls, dance halls, and gambling—gave the Filipinos a bad reputation. But they were the only outlets the Filipinos had. They were not allowed to take part in the recreations of white society. They had all experienced the humiliation and violence of racism, even the women and children. To be safe, they had to stick to the ghetto and its pursuits.

The Forgotten Filipinos   The Filipinos remained very isolated from whites. No one knew very much about them or cared about their problems. They are often called the "forgotten Filipinos." They found ways to help each other through their churches and families.

Their Catholic churches were a kind of welfare agency for the Filipinos. The church helped the immigrants find housing and work. It also helped them improve their social conditions. For example, the church started Bible-study groups and literary societies for young people. These groups promoted literacy and education among the Filipinos.

The Filipinos liked to play baseball and go fishing. They also took comfort in folk dancing, music, and festivals. They formed folk dancing societies to teach their dances to children. Fiestas gave them a chance to mingle with old friends and to remember and celebrate their culture. Those Filipinos who did

A Filipino American family outing in the 1930s

marry formed large extended families here. These families usually included many unmarried male friends who acted as "uncles" to the children. Events such as marriages, christenings, and funerals allowed members of the family to get together.

Filipino Men and Intermarriage   In 1930, 80 percent of the Filipinos in California were men under the age of thirty. The ratio of Filipino men to Filipino women in the state was 14 to 1. The few Filipino women who came to the United States had to work hard as maids or field hands. When it came to marrying, however, they had a wide choice of eligible men. Each Filipino woman usually had several ardent suitors.

Still, there were few Filipino women to marry. The men began to marry women from other minorities, such as Chinese, Japanese, and Mexicans. Filipinos and Mexicans had much in common. They shared the Spanish language and the same religion. They were both members of downtrodden minorities.

Even more Filipinos married white women. These couples encountered great difficulties. The Filipinos came from a culture in which mixed-race marriages were common and accepted. They found it difficult to understand the attitudes they encountered in the United States.

AMERICAN CONTRADICTIONS

To Filipinos, America often was difficult to understand. They found many contradictions. Americans said one thing but did the opposite. They spoke of equality but treated Filipinos as inferiors. They bragged about opportunity but allowed Filipinos to do only the most difficult and undesirable jobs. One American could be unspeakably cruel and racist, the next brimming with kindness. Filipinos began to question the beautiful image of America they had learned about in school. Here is how one young Filipino writer saw the country:

> *Where is the heart of America? I am one of many thousands of young men, born under the American flag, raised as loyal, idealistic Americans under your promise of equality for all, and enticed by glowing tales of educational opportunities. Once here we are met by exploiters, shunted into slums, greeted only by gamblers and prostitutes, taught only the worst in civilization. America came to us with bright-winged promises of liberty, equality, fraternity. What has become of them?*
> —*Manuel Buaken*
>
> As quoted in Linda Perrin, *Coming to America: Immigrants from the Far East* (New York: Delacorte, 1980), p. 123.

WORLD WAR II

It was Sunday morning, December 7, 1941, in Pearl Harbor, Hawaii. Most people were just getting up or were still in bed. Suddenly Japanese warplanes came roaring out of the sky. They dropped hundreds of bombs and torpedoes on the

American fleet anchored in the harbor. The Japanese attack on Pearl Harbor sank or damaged nineteen ships and killed 2,300 Americans. On that day, the United States entered World War II.

Seven hours later, the Japanese bombed Clark Field. This American army airfield was in northern Luzon in the Philippines. All in one day, Americans and Filipinos found themselves fighting side by side for their homelands and for democracy. It was a day that would bring about great changes for the United States, for the Philippines, and for Filipino immigrants.

General MacArthur had not yet had time to build a strong Philippine military force. Caught off guard, he and his American and Filipino troops were forced to retreat from Manila. They went to the Bataan Peninsula and the island of Corregidor in Manila Bay.

There, the Filipinos and Americans fought valiantly to hold the Japanese. The U.S. government evacuated MacArthur from Bataan. He was sent to Australia. There, he was given the job of retaking the Philippines. When he arrived in Australia, MacArthur promised the people of the Philippines, "I shall return."

The Bataan Death March   The American and Filipino troops held out on Bataan for four months. The Americans were impressed with the bravery and abilities of the Filipinos.

After the fall of Bataan, the Japanese forced 80,000 Americans and Filipinos to march 120 miles to prison camps in San Fernando. At the end of each day, the Japanese killed all those who could not walk any farther. This march came to be known as the Bataan death march. It lasted six days. Later, thousands of Filipinos and Americans died in Japanese prison camps from starvation, disease, and torture. This experience forged a special bond between the Filipino and American survivors of the Japanese invasion.

Occupation and Resistance   The Japanese occupied the Philippines for most of the rest of the war. During that occupation, more than 1 million Filipinos died. Some died of starvation, others from bombing, and still others from the treatment they received from the Japanese. Hundreds of thousands of Filipinos escaped into the hills and became resistance fighters. They attacked Japanese supply lines and outposts and sabotaged Japanese operations. The freedom fighters also sent information to MacArthur about Japanese movements.

Changing Attitudes   American attitudes toward Filipinos changed dramatically during the war. Americans greatly admired the Filipino soldiers and freedom fighters. Now America's "little brown brothers" were no longer savages and "boys." They were men, allies, and heroes. Americans sympathized with the Filipinos who were suffering through the Japanese occupation. They began to treat Filipinos in the United States more humanely.

Working in Defense Plants   The war ended the Great Depression. All of a sudden, workers were needed to fill thousands of jobs in American shipyards, weapons factories, and aircraft plants. These factories turned out ships, planes, guns, and tanks to aid the American war effort. The anti-Filipino rioting ended. In 1942, President Franklin Roosevelt signed an executive order to allow Filipinos to work in the defense plants. This was an important milestone for Filipino Americans. For the first time, Filipinos were able to work in white-collar jobs. They became clerks, engineers, and technicians.

In the Armed Forces   Many Filipinos, however, wanted to join the armed forces and fight for the liberation of their homeland. More than 80,000 Filipinos rushed to enlist in the army and navy after Pearl Harbor. They were rejected because they were still only U.S. nationals, not citizens. According to the federal draft law, only resident aliens and citizens could enlist. The Filipinos made a great outcry over this. As a result, President Roosevelt had the enlistment regulations changed to include them.

Two Filipino U.S. Army regiments fought in the South Pacific and helped liberate the Philippines. Many Filipino soldiers were used to spy and commit sabotage behind enemy lines. They looked like other natives, and they knew the jungles and mountains. These men were so brave that forty-four of them received Bronze Stars.

MacArthur was not able to keep his promise to return until 1944. When he left his landing craft and came walking through the waves onto a Philippine beach, Filipinos were overjoyed. The liberation of the Philippines had begun. However, the liberation took time. More Filipinos were killed in action during the retaking of the islands than in the original invasion.

General Douglas MacArthur (1880–1964) (left) returning to the Philippines, 1944

Independence and Immigration, 1946–1990

PHILIPPINE INDEPENDENCE

In 1946, after the ten-year transition period provided in the Tydings-McDuffie Act and a one-year delay because of the war, the American government kept its word and granted independence to the Philippines. A separate law also allowed Filipinos to become naturalized American citizens. That may not have been the best time for the United States to let go of the Philippines. The war had devastated the islands. Eighty percent of Manila lay in ruins. The war had also destroyed the island's economy.

Some people felt that the United States should not have counted the war years as part of the transition period. They wanted the federal government to give the Philippines five more years to recover. Others argued that if the United States postponed independence, it would appear to have gone back on its word.

The Philippines became an independent nation on July 4, 1946. The U.S. government had wanted the Philippines to gain its independence on America's own independence day. However, the Philippines celebrate June 12 as Philippine Independence Day. That is the anniversary of the day the Philippines declared its independence from Spain in 1898. July 4 is celebrated as Philippine-American Friendship Day.

IMMIGRATION FROM 1946 TO 1965

Filipino immigration to the United States soared after World War II. Between 1940 and 1960, the number of Filipinos residing in the United States nearly quadrupled. Those who came between 1946 and 1965 are often referred to as the "second wave."

FILIPINO AMERICAN POPULATION, 1910–1960*

1910	406
1920	5,603
1930	45,208
1940	45,876
1950	61,645
1960	181,614

Source: U.S. Census.
*Only 1960 figure includes Hawaii (69,070).

Who came? After the war, many Filipinos came to the United States looking for work. These included professionals and skilled and unskilled workers.

During the prewar period, more men had come than women. Now more women came than men. Some were war brides, others were the wives of earlier immigrants. Still others were independent migrants. This enabled Filipino immigrants to begin marrying and having children. For the first time, Filipinos produced a large number of second-generation Filipino Americans.

WHY DID THE SECOND WAVE COME?

After the war, the Philippines was slow to recover. The farms and ranches did not produce as much as before the war. And the fishing fleet and railroads had been destroyed. In addition, the Philippines was still made up of a few rich families who owned most of the land and millions of poor, landless peasants.

While conditions remained bad at home, they had greatly improved for Filipinos in the United States. Thanks to the war, people treated Filipinos better. There were more and better jobs. Right after the war, then, more Filipinos came to the United States to have better lives.

THE IMMIGRATION ACT OF 1965

In 1965 Congress passed a new law that made it much easier for Filipinos and other Asians to immigrate to the United States. Along with the Civil Rights Act of 1964 and the Voting Rights Act of 1965, the new immigration law reflected the country's new liberal attitude in these matters. The Immigration Act of 1965 removed national quotas. Under the new law, 170,000 people could immigrate each year from the Eastern Hemisphere. That included Europe, Africa, and Asia. As many as 20,000 people could come from any one country.

Since 1965, the Filipino American population has risen more than five times.

FILIPINO AMERICAN POPULATION, 1970–1990*

1970	336,731
1980	774,652
1985	1,051,600 (est.)
1990	1,405,146 (est.)

Source: U.S. Census.
*Including Hawaii.

Filipinos are expected to be the largest Asian group in the United States by the end of the century. (Chinese are the second largest.) In the 1980s, three-quarters of all Filipino residents were immigrants.

Filipinos who have come to the United States since the 1965 immigration law was enacted are called the third wave. They differed from earlier immigrants. They came from urban rather than rural areas. Most came to settle permanently in the United States, not as sojourners. Sixty percent became citizens within five to eight years of their arrival.

THE THIRD WAVE: WHY DID IT HAPPEN?

Economic Reasons   Two-thirds of the most recent Filipino arrivals are trained in health professions. They are doctors, nurses, optometrists, veterinarians, pharmacists, and dietitians. Other kinds of professionals also came. They include lawyers, engineers, and architects.

The new law allowed Filipino citizens and permanent aliens to bring family members over. As in the second wave, more women than men came. From 1966 to 1971, 66,517 Filipino women and 47,599 men arrived in the United States. Most of the women were trained in a profession. Even more than in other Asian groups, Filipino women expected to work in their professions here in the United States.

These people came because there were few jobs for professionals back home. Philippine universities were producing more doctors, lawyers, and engineers than there were jobs for. Those who did have jobs had to work for very low wages.

> *There is an overabundance of a well-*
> *educated middle class in the Philippines. . . .*
> *Only 60 percent of today's college graduates*
> *are employed in any more than menial jobs.*
> —*Jack Foisie,* Los Angeles Times, *1972*

42

*Wages in Manila are barely enough to
answer for my family's needs. I must go
abroad to better my chances.*
                              —*an immigrant*

*My one day's earning here in America is
more than my one month's salary in
Manila.*
                                  —*a nurse*

*In the United States, hard work is rewarded.
In the Philippines, it is part of the struggle to
survive.*
                              —*an accountant*

As quoted in Ronald Takaki, *Strangers from a
Different Shore: A History of Asian Americans*
(Boston: Little, Brown, 1989), p. 433.

Political Reasons   After the Philippines was granted
independence, it became a democracy based largely on the
American model. Presidents were limited to two four-year
terms. From 1946 to 1965, the Philippines had several presidents of varying abilities. Some were corrupt. Others tried to
govern well. Not one was able to bring about adequate land
reform. In the meantime, Communist guerrillas and Muslim
separatists who wanted their own nation began fighting the
government in parts of the Philippines.

In 1965, Ferdinand Marcos was elected president of the
Philippines. At first he was popular because he was able to
carry out a small land-reform program. He also built roads,
schools, and bridges. However, in the late 1960s, he tried to
change the form of government to a parliamentary democracy.
This change would have enabled him to remain in office as
leader indefinitely instead of for only eight years.

The Philippines Loses Its Freedoms   Opposition to
Marcos began to grow. In 1972, Marcos declared martial law,
although historians agree that there was no basis for it. He

Ferdinand Marcos (1917–1989) with his wife Imelda (1929–) at a rally for his seventieth birthday

suspended the Philippine constitution and civil rights. He also arrested many of his opponents. Under martial law, there were no national elections. As "temporary president," Marcos continued in office until 1986.

One leader who opposed him was Senator Benigno Aquino. Marcos imprisoned Aquino for eight years. Finally, he allowed Aquino to go into exile in the United States. Marcos lifted martial law in 1981. Two years later, he allowed Aquino to return. As Aquino stepped off an airplane in Manila, a gunman shot him dead. Marcos's men then shot and killed the assassin. Later, it was learned that twenty-six government agents had been involved in a conspiracy to kill Aquino. None were ever convicted.

The world was horrified by Aquino's murder. In 1986, opposition leaders persuaded his widow, Corazon Aquino, to run for president. She received the most votes. However, the National Assembly controlled by Marcos named Marcos the winner. Nine days later, the Philippine people staged an uprising. Marcos was forced to flee to the United States. On February 25, 1986, Corazon Aquino was sworn in as president.

After Marcos went into exile, people discovered that he and his wife Imelda had stolen money. They had taken several billion dollars from the Philippine government and from foreign aid that the United States had given to the Philippines.

The troubles of the Marcos period led many people to leave the Philippines for the United States. Many middle-class professional people feared being imprisoned and tortured by the Marcos regime. Others left because they could not get jobs or go to school unless they "knew someone" in Marcos's corrupt government.

Democracy Restored Corazon Aquino has restored democracy to the Filipino people. She has tried to revive the nation's economy and bring about some further land reform. The problems of extreme poverty remain. She has not been able to control the army or subdue the Communist guerrillas. As a result, she has had to fight off several attempts to overthrow her government.

Corazon Aquino (1932–) speaking at a military ceremony

OCCUPATIONS OF FILIPINO AMERICANS

Still in the Navy   Filipinos have been serving in the U.S. Navy since the early 1900s. Joining the navy has always been an important way for Filipinos to immigrate to the United States. In 1930, 25,000 Filipinos were serving in the navy. For decades, Filipinos were only allowed to be stewards. In effect, they were servants for white officers and men, a form of segregation. They were cooks, valets, waiters, and butlers. After World War II, the United States allowed Filipinos who had served three years in the navy to apply for citizenship. After the navy was formally desegregated in the late 1940s, Filipinos were allowed to do other jobs.

Filipino American sailors, like this yeoman, now work at many jobs.

Since 1947, 2,000 volunteers from the Philippines have been allowed to enlist in the navy each year. After they have finished their service, they may immigrate to the United States and become citizens. Many choose to stay in the navy and make it their lifelong career. In 1983, the navy had 19,733 Filipino enlisted men and 379 officers. Like other military retirees, many Filipinos settle in towns and cities near naval bases when they leave the navy.

Doctors and Nurses   As noted, many Filipino doctors and nurses have immigrated to the United States. They serve in hospitals all over the country. In the 1950s and 1960s, the U.S. government started a foreign-exchange program for doctors and nurses. Doctors and nurses from other countries were encouraged to come to the United States for training. They were expected to take what they learned here back to their own countries. Nearly 90 percent of the doctors and nurses who signed up for the program were Filipino. Many of them did not go back home when their training was finished.

In the 1970s, one-fifth of all nurses who graduated from nursing schools in the Philippines came to the United States. Only about one-third of them went back. In 1974, there were 7,000 Filipino American doctors in the United States. About 1,000 of them settled in New York City, which had a Filipino American population of 45,000. Today Filipino American doctors are on the staffs of nearly every hospital in New York and New Jersey.

Filipino American doctors and nurses have made important contributions to American medicine. During the 1980s, most hospitals suffered from a nursing shortage. Thousands of Filipino American nurses helped fill the void. Hospitals have also suffered from a shortage of doctors. Most doctors want to start their own practices instead of working in a hospital. Many Filipino American doctors have taken hospital jobs.

Filipino Americans are health professionals in many hospitals.

Overcoming Obstacles Doctors and nurses and other professionals encounter many problems when they come to the United States. Most of them have to pass tests to qualify to work here. If they fail the tests, they have to go back to medical school. Some have had to take temporary jobs as cooks, taxi drivers, laboratory assistants, and nurse's aides. It is common to find a Filipino doctor working as a nurse's aide or a nurse working as a salesclerk.

Testing and licensing procedures have kept many immigrants from working in other professions as well. Thousands of teachers, veterinarians, lawyers, and engineers have all been shut out of their professions. Many people are now demanding changes in licensing laws. These laws were established originally both to protect professional standards in the United States and to protect jobs. People feel that the laws are being used to exclude qualified immigrants to protect American workers.

Still on the Farm   A great many Filipino immigrants still work in agriculture in the western states. Filipinos and Mexican immigrants are still willing to perform backbreaking stoop labor in the farm fields. Most Americans do not want to do these jobs.

Life in the fields has gotten better for Filipino workers. One reason for this is that the workers have become unionized. In the 1960s, a Filipino, Larry Itliong, organized thousands of Filipino farm workers. They formed the Agricultural Workers Organizing Committee (AWOC).

Itliong's union went on strike against thirty-one grape growers in the San Joaquin Valley in 1965. A week later, the National Farm Workers Organization (NFWO) joined the strikers. The NFWO was a union of Mexican American farm workers organized by Cesar Chavez. The strike and a nation-wide grape boycott lasted four and a half years. Nearly 17 million Americans boycotted grapes and California wine. The strike was successful. The two unions won better pay and working conditions for their members. The unions merged in 1967 and became the United Farm Workers union.

Larry Itliong (1914– 1977), organizer of the AWOC

HOW DO FILIPINO AMERICANS
THINK OF THEMSELVES?

Their families and the regions they come from are still as important to recent Filipino immigrants as they were to older immigrants. When two Filipinos meet in the United States, they immediately exchange information. They tell where they are from, what language they speak, and who their family members are. Many of them belong to social clubs and organizations based on their Filipino origins. They keep close ties with family members back home. They continue to send money to their family groups. They go home to visit often.

Loyal Americans Because the Philippines was once an American colony, Filipino immigrants come to the United States already feeling like Americans. They arrive knowing how to speak English. They are striving very hard to fit in, to become Americans and to achieve the American dream. Many Filipinos resent not being considered loyal Americans. They are very proud of their sacrifices during World War II.

A Proud Minority Filipinos have been nearly invisible to most Americans. People mistake them for Chinese, Japanese, and Mexicans. They are most often taken for Hispanics because of their Spanish surnames and because many of them speak Spanish. But the Filipinos are proud of their culture and heritage. They want to be recognized as Filipinos. The most recent immigrants, who are middle-class professionals, have tried to separate themselves from older immigrants. They think of the older immigrants as working-class, nonprofessional Filipinos. The newcomers especially dislike being called Pinoys. They want to be called Filipino Americans.

Like so many immigrants before them, Filipino Americans do not always find life in the United States easy. But like the others, they will find their own successful place in the American mosaic.

50

OUTSTANDING FILIPINO AMERICANS

Carlos Bulosan

Carlos Bulosan (1913–1956) was a Filipino American poet and writer. He was born in Luzon. Bulosan came to the United States in 1930, when he was seventeen. He worked in a fish cannery and as a houseboy, dishwasher, and field hand.

As a boy in the Philippines, Bulosan learned English and studied about America. His hero was Abraham Lincoln, a poor boy who grew up to be president. Bulosan arrived in the United States just as the depression was beginning. He experienced much of the racism and violence that many Filipinos suffered during those hard times. At one point, a mob tarred and feathered him and chased him out of town.

Bulosan felt the need to write about his experiences and those of other Filipinos in the United States. He began writing for a labor newspaper. In 1946, his book, *America Is in the Heart,* was published. In it he told of his search for the ideal America he had learned about in school and the real, sometimes harsh, America he had found when he came to the United States.

G. Monty Manibog

G. Monty Manibog's experiences were very different from those of Carlos Bulosan. He immigrated later and was a professional person. Manibog was born in 1930 in the Philippines. He grew up in Hawaii. His father was a lawyer. When Manibog was a teenager, his father took his family back to the Philippines. Manibog attended the University of the Philippines. Then he served in the U.S. Army. After the army, he graduated from Loyola University Law School in New Orleans.

Manibog settled in Monterey Park, California, in 1961. Monterey Park is a largely Chinese American suburban community. Many wealthy and middle-class Chinese Americans live there. Manibog was elected to the Monterey Park City Council in 1976. Two years later, he was elected mayor of Monterey Park. He married and has six children.

Manibog has continued to practice law. Many Filipino immigrants go to him for legal help when they get in trouble with the law or with immigration authorities.

Maniya "Honey" Barredo

Maniya Barredo is a ballerina with the Atlanta Ballet. She was born in Manila in 1952. In the Philippines, Barredo was a star. She danced before visiting presidents. When she was eighteen, her mother sent her to the United States to study ballet. It was very hard for Barredo to adjust to a new culture. It was also hard to keep up with her difficult classes at the Joffrey Ballet School. When she compared herself to her classmates, she felt less advanced. Although she wanted to quit and go back to the Philippines, her mother and her ballet teacher encouraged her to keep trying.

Since then, she has performed with many outstanding ballet companies. In 1977, she became the prima ballerina of the Atlanta Ballet. She has worked with some of the greatest dancers in the world, such as Russian American Mikhail Baryshnikov.

She has also received international acclaim. Yet she finds teaching summer ballet classes for children in Manila to be just as rewarding as her fame. She once told a class, "The reason why I share what I know with you is because this is what love is all about. We should all share and reach for a goal." She has surely reached that goal herself.

FILIPINO RELIGION

Here in the United States, religion has continued to be an important part of Filipino life. The majority are still Roman Catholic. Some are Muslim, and a few are Protestant. The Christianity of the majority is one trait that Filipinos share with most Americans.

For many Filipinos, the rituals of the Catholic church are also important family occasions. The christening of a new baby calls for a large, happy party for family and friends. Filipino parents choose close friends to be the baby's godparents. Godparents are supposed to be responsible for a child's religious training if something happens to the parents. In Filipino families, the godparents are very important. They become lifelong members of the baby's family group. They share all of the rights and responsibilities of the group.

Christian holidays are joyous events for most Filipinos. Easter is a very important holiday among Catholic Filipinos. Christmas lasts from December 16 to December 25 with masses and church processions. The "fiesta season" runs from January 6 to January 16 with additional processions and church services. The Feast of Santo Niño ("Holy Child") is the highlight of the fiesta season. Church members stage a procession through the community carrying a statue of the Christ Child. Then the statue is taken back to the church, where religious services are held.

This Filipino American baby is dressed in an elaborate lace gown for the christening ceremony in church.

The Feast of Santo Niño ("Holy Child") is the highlight of the fiesta season in January.

FESTIVALS

In the Philippines, the people frequently hold celebrations and festivals. The festivities give the people a chance to forget about their poverty and hard work. In addition to their religious festivals, Filipinos celebrate harvest time and several national holidays. In the United States, festivals are a way for Filipino Americans to remember and celebrate their culture and heritage.

Filipinos and Filipino Americans celebrate December 30 as Rizal Day. This is when Filipinos remember their national hero, José Rizal. The holiday is held on the anniversary of the day that the Spanish executed Rizal in 1896. Filipino American groups also celebrate Philippine Independence Day on June 12 and Philippine-American Friendship Day on July 4.

In the United States, some Filipino social clubs and organizations stage annual cultural festivals. The men dress in tribal costumes. The women wear Filipino dresses trimmed in fine lace. Bands play Filipino musical instruments and sing folk songs. Dance troupes perform intricate folk dances such as the *tinikling*. In this dance, dancers have to step in and out quickly from between moving bamboo poles. People can sample Filipino foods and buy arts and crafts at the festivals.

FILIPINO FOOD

The Spanish, the Chinese, and the Malays have all contributed to Filipino cooking. As it is in other Asian countries, rice is the main staple of the Philippines. Many Filipino dishes are made of chopped meat mixed with vegetables, rice, and spicy sauces. Filipino cooks use ginger, garlic, soy sauce, and coconut milk to season their dishes. Seafood, such as shrimp, cuttlefish, and mussels, is an important part of the Filipino diet. Filipinos also eat a lot of beef, pork, chicken, and noodles.

Filipino Dishes   *Adobo* is a national dish of the Philippines. It is a dark, tangy stew. Adobo is made from chicken, pork, octopus, and vegetables cooked with vinegar, pepper, and garlic. Children buy *balut,* a favorite snack, from street vendors. It is a boiled duck egg that was ready to hatch. Snackers can see beaks and feathers when they break open the shell. Another national dish is *lechon.* This is suckling pig served in a thick liver sauce. Lechon is usually served at festivals and celebrations.

Adobo

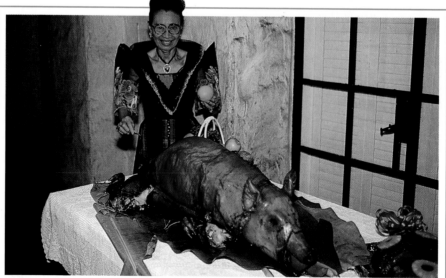

Roast pig, as served in the Philippines

Staff members of the *Filipino Reporter* at work in New York City

THE FILIPINO AMERICAN PRESS

Filipino American newspapers have been a big factor in helping Filipinos adapt to life in the United States. The first students, the pensionados, started a newsletter called the *Filipino Student Bulletin.* This small newspaper was published for nearly twenty years. It gave students news and advice and helped them stay in touch with one another.

Since then, dozens of Filipino American newspapers have been published in the United States. Most last about seven years. In 1976, Filipino Americans were publishing nineteen newspapers, eight newsletters, and one magazine in the United States. All of them were in English. Nine of the publishers were located in California.

Several Filipino newspapers thrive in Hawaii and California and in other western states. Typically they print news about the Philippines and about Filipinos that other newspapers do not cover. They cover activities of the Filipino organizations. They also announce weddings, births, christenings, and community events.

FILIPINO AMERICAN ORGANIZATIONS

Filipino immigrants have formed hundreds of social and mutual-aid organizations. Each club represents a region or province of the Philippines. Immigrants join the club that represents their villages back home. In the club they can speak their own language and even find friends and relatives who have also emigrated from the Philippines.

Filipino immigrants also have two large organizations that take in all Filipinos. These are the Caballeros de Dimas Alang and the Legionarios del Trabajo. These two groups provide help and friendship for Filipino Americans. They have built hospitals and homes for the aged. They help immigrants learn better English, find jobs and housing, and start businesses.

The social clubs helped Filipinos survive the Great Depression. They also provided a haven where Filipinos could feel safe from discrimination. Today they act as substitute families for immigrants and help keep Filipino culture alive.

PROBLEMS FOR FILIPINO AMERICAN FAMILIES

Filipino American families face many problems. In the Philippines, each Filipino has the support and help of an extended family to overcome problems. Here, Filipinos do not have such large family groups to depend on. They have to learn to ask government agencies and their churches for help. As with other immigrant groups, their American-born children go to American schools. They dress and act like other American children. They have the same hopes and face the same obstacles. Education is still extremely important to Filipino families.

American-born Filipinos are not as aware of their heritage and culture as their parents. In Filipino families, children are expected to be obedient. Filipino parents are shocked when

Filipino American teenagers adapt easily to the American life-style.

their Americanized children talk back to them. They are shocked too when their teenagers, like many American teens, become involved with drugs and alcohol.

MAKING IT IN AMERICA

Despite their education, Filipino immigrants lag behind other Asian immigrant groups economically. Many, even those with good educations and abilities, are forced to remain in low-paying jobs. The 1980 census found that Filipino men earned only about two-thirds as much as white men. It also showed that very few Filipinos worked in high-level jobs or went into business for themselves.

Racial discrimination is one reason Filipinos cannot get better jobs. Many companies will not promote them to management jobs because they do not want to put them in charge of white workers. However, conditions have improved for Filipinos in the last twenty-five years. Federal and state laws bar discrimination in hiring and housing. Filipinos can eat in any restaurant and stay at any hotel they choose. They are able to live in nice city neighborhoods and in middle-class suburbs. Filipino organizations are banding together to fight unfair licensing laws that keep professionals out of good jobs. Filipinos are also becoming more involved in politics. This will help them win more rights for their people.

MAINTAINING LINKS TO THE PAST

Today's Filipino Americans maintain close ties to the old country. They write to family and friends. They subscribe to Philippine newspapers and magazines. Many can afford to fly back to the Philippines frequently.

The Philippine government has encouraged Filipino Americans to return to the Philippines. It wants them to come back as tourists and spend money in the Philippines. It also wants well-educated Filipinos to move back and help build the nation.

However, most Filipinos are still going the other way. Poverty and lack of opportunities in the Philippines still force immigrants to come to the United States in great numbers. Jonalo Ace Chua, a columnist for a Philippine newspaper, recently wrote: "The Philippines, with all its natural wealth, is an enormous prison of poverty, and most everyone who can escape from it finds it hard to pass up the chance. Many believe that the American dream can only be realized in America. Somehow, they have the idea that they're gonna make it in America! And make it big!"

Many Filipino American families have overcome poverty and are enjoying their new lives in the United States.

**Dancers at a Filipino American festival in California
dancing the *tinikling*, which is performed among
moving bamboo poles**

SOURCES

Cordova, Fred. *Filipinos: Forgotten Asian Americans.* Dubuque, Iowa: Kendall, 1983.

Crouchett, Lorraine Jacobs. *Filipinos in California: From the Days of the Galleons to the Present.* El Cerrito, Calif.: Downey Place, 1982.

Daniels, Roger. *Coming to America: A History of Immigration and Ethnicity in American Life.* New York: Harper & Row, 1990.

Gardner, Robert W.; Bryant Robey; and Peter C. Smith. "Asian Americans: Growth, Change and Diversity." *Population Bulletin,* vol. 40, no. 4, October 1985.

Kitano, Harry H. L., and Roger Daniels. *Asian Americans: Emerging Minorities.* Englewood Cliffs, N.J.: Prentice-Hall, 1988.

Knoll, Patricia. *Becoming Americans.* Portland, Ore.: Coast to Coast Books, 1982.

Perrin, Linda. *Coming to America: Immigrants from the Far East.* New York: Delacorte, 1980.

Pido, Antonio J. A. *The Pilipinos in America.* New York: Center for Migration Studies, 1986.

Takaki, Ronald. *Strangers from a Different Shore: A History of Asian Americans.* Boston: Little, Brown, 1989.

Thernstrom, Stephan, ed. *Harvard Encyclopedia of American Ethnic Groups.* Cambridge: Harvard University Press, 1980.

INDEX